Lily Lolek
Future Saint

by Katie Warner

illustrated by Amy Rodriguez

Text copyright © 2020 Katie Warner
Illustrations copyright © 2020 Amy Rodriguez

All rights reserved. With the exception of short excerpts used in critical review, no part of this work may be reproduced, transmitted, or stored in any form whatsoever, without the prior written permission of the publisher.

Book design by Meg Whalen.
The text for this book is set in Belda and Spumante.
The illustrations for this book were rendered digitally.

ISBN: 978-1-5051-1656-4

Published in the United States by
TAN Books
PO Box 269
Gastonia, NC 28053
www.TANBooks.com

Printed in the United States of America

For Meg — Thanks for being my best book buddy
and raising future saints alongside me.
— K.W.

To my parents. Thank you for teaching me how to aspire to holiness.
— A.R.

This is the story of Lily Lolek.
There was nothing that she wanted more
than to love with her might and to burst with God's joy
'til the day she reached heaven's big door.

She would sweep and then read and play down by the creek —

pretend to be *Damien* helping the weak,

thinking like *Thomas* until the sun set,

honoring Mary like *Saint Bernadette*.

She'd be like *Elizabeth* feeding the poor.

Pretend to be famous *King David* in war,

Scholastica, loving her brother to bits,

and Philip with his most playful of wits.

"I'll be a *saint* in God's family someday!"
"You'll never be like them," one girl dared to say.
"But why not?" Lily thought, confused and perplexed.
She hung her head low, plodded home sad and vexed.

Still Lily kept dreaming
and humming a tune
the saints on her mind,
in hand - book and broom.

She imagined and played until late one spring day
Father Michael came by for a dinnertime stay.
"I've a question for you," the priest asked Lily.
"When you grow up, do you know what you'll be?"

Lily took a deep breath and she started to speak
Of all the saints lives she read down by the creek —

She pretended to fight like Saint Joan of Arc,
Cared for creatures, like Francis, until it was dark.
Like Maria Goretti,
 she stood against sin.
Like Augustine,
 she never let heresy win.
She set an example
 like Saint Dominic,
  being kind, helping others,
   even when sick.

Lily spoke out her dreams
and danced 'round the room.
Like Saint Martin de Porres,
she held tight to her broom.

"Here's the thing, Father," young Lily replied.
"I've learned about so many saints who've since died...
They did marvelous things that I just can't repeat.
How could I ever have their good deeds beat?

They're great thinkers and speakers and great soldiers, too.
They could make the poor happy when they felt so blue.
They fasted, they travelled, they prayed, healed the lame.
Their lives were so great — How could mine be the same?"

"Well, well, my child," Father Michael then said.
"You've got an idea that is wrong in your head.
God doesn't want a new *Jane* or *Thérèse*.
He wants someone else now — He wants YOU instead.

He gave you some gifts no one else can repeat,
your own unique heart, mind and soul, hands and feet.
He wants you to use them in your special way
to become the saint that He needs for *today*.

"There's no mold and
no checklist,
no just one right way
to be a saint
up in heaven someday.
You're free to become
who God made you to be,
and you're already
on the right track,
can't you see?"

"You're a dreamer, a joyful young child who loves,
filled with wonder and smiles and big ol' bear hugs.
Your laughter, your playing — it all makes God smile.
Right here God wants you to stay for a while —
To live your life like only you, Lily, can.
No need to come up with a grand, foolproof plan.
He'll guide you and lead you, through prayer and with trust,
to the kind of life that makes sparkles from dust."

"Be you poor — rich — slow — smart —
strong or weak — scared to start,
He put you here at this great moment in time
to write your own story, to make your own rhyme,
to dream your own dream of how best to serve Him,
to race the good race only you, child, can win."

"Miss Lily, you're loved for just who you are.
The saints are examples of how to go far
in loving and serving and being your best,
but their stories aren't yours; you're on your own quest.

This good news is freeing, so hopeful and true...
perhaps you know now just what you have to do...?"

"I have to be ME!" shouted little Lily.
"To be just the saint God made me to be!
What adventure,
what challenge,
what beauty and fun...
I must finish dinner! There's work to be done!"

"To love my dear Jesus more and more everyday.
To take less and to give a whole lot more away.

To grow in virtue and to stay far from sin.
To learn that my life is all about *Him*.

Sure I'll make some mistakes, perhaps quite a bit.
But just like the saints, what I won't do is quit.
And by using my own unique heart, soul and mind...

"I'll be Saint Lily Lolek, one-of-a-kind."

So from that day to this,
you'll find this sweet girl
down by the creek
and out in the world,
with a broom in her hand
and a book from her shelf,
loving God with abandon,
just being herself.

Lily's Litany

Here is Lily's litany — you can make one, too!
You can learn about the saints and have them pray for you.
If you follow in their footsteps, loving God most faithfully,
you'll become the special kind of saint that He made YOU to be!

Saint Damien of Molochi, *pray for us!*
Saint Thomas Aquinas, *pray for us!*
Mary, Mother of God, Queen of Saints, *pray for us!*
Saint Bernadette of Lourdes, *pray for us!*
Saint Elizabeth of Hungary, *pray for us!*
King David from Sacred Scripture, *pray for us!*
Saint Scholastica, sister of Saint Benedict, *pray for us!*
Saint Philip Neri, *pray for us!*
Saint Joan of Arc, *pray for us!*
Saint Francis of Assisi, *pray for us!*
Saint Maria Goretti, *pray for us!*
Saint Augustine of Hippo, *pray for us!*
Saint Dominic Savio, *pray for us!*
Saint Martin de Porres, *pray for us!*
Saint Jane Frances de Chantal, *pray for us!*
Saint Therese of Lisieux, *pray for us!*

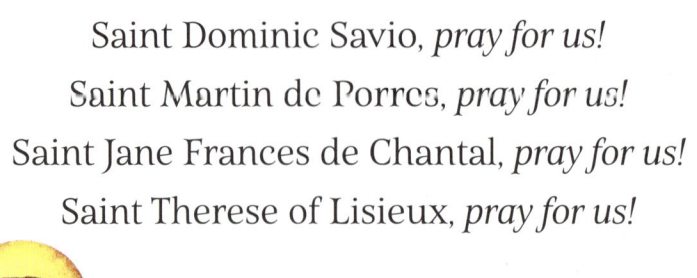